Musick of the Fifes & Drums
Volume Four

An Instructor for the Drum

by John C. Moon
Musickmaster

The Colonial Williamsburg Foundation
Williamsburg, Virginia

© 1981 by The Colonial Williamsburg Foundation
Library of Congress Cataloging in Publication Data

ISBN 0-87935-059-8 (instruction manual)

ISBN 0-87935-060-1 (instruction manual and record)

Printed in the United States of America

Library of Congress Cataloging in Publication Data

Moon, John C
  An instructor for the drum.

  (Musick of the fifes & drums; v. 4)
  At head of title: Virginia State Garrison Regiment of Williamsburg.
  1. Drum—Methods. I. Colonial Williamsburg Foundation. II. Virginia State
Garrison Regiment of Williamsburg. III. Title. IV. Series: Musick of the fifes and
drums; v. 4.
M1270.M94   vol. 4   [MT662.2]   785.1′3s   80-29134
ISBN 0-87935-059-8   [789′.1′071]

Table of Contents

Preface

This booklet should be used in conjunction with the long playing record that contains the lessons in rudiments. Only the rudiments and repertoire lessons have been recorded. Care must be taken, however, to insure that the student does not neglect the other lessons in this booklet that explain theory and symbols. A drummer who cannot read is incomplete and will meet restrictions throughout his musical career. The lessons contained herein are in chronological order, and the student should not proceed to the next lesson until he is satisfied with his understanding and execution of the current one.

The drum, an ancient instrument of eastern origin, is used militarily for communication: it is a signal instrument as well as a musical accompaniment for other instruments. A percussion instrument of different styles, basically a drum consists of a skin or pairs of skins stretched over a sound box made of varying materials that is struck by sticks, mallets, hands, or fingers to produce an indefinite pitch.

Three types of drums were in general use by the military prior to and during the colonial period. The side or snare drum, which has two heads, is played only on the upper, or batter, head, while the bass drum, with two heads, is carried across the chest and is played on both sides. As befitted eighteenth-century infantry units, the Fifes and Drums of Colonial Williamsburg play only the wooden-shelled snare and bass drums. *The Instructor for the Drum* will not treat the kettle drum, which is made of copper or brass, has only one head, and can produce definite pitches. Usually employed in pairs, kettle drums are normally used by cavalry units.

LESSON ONE
The Parts of a Snare Drum

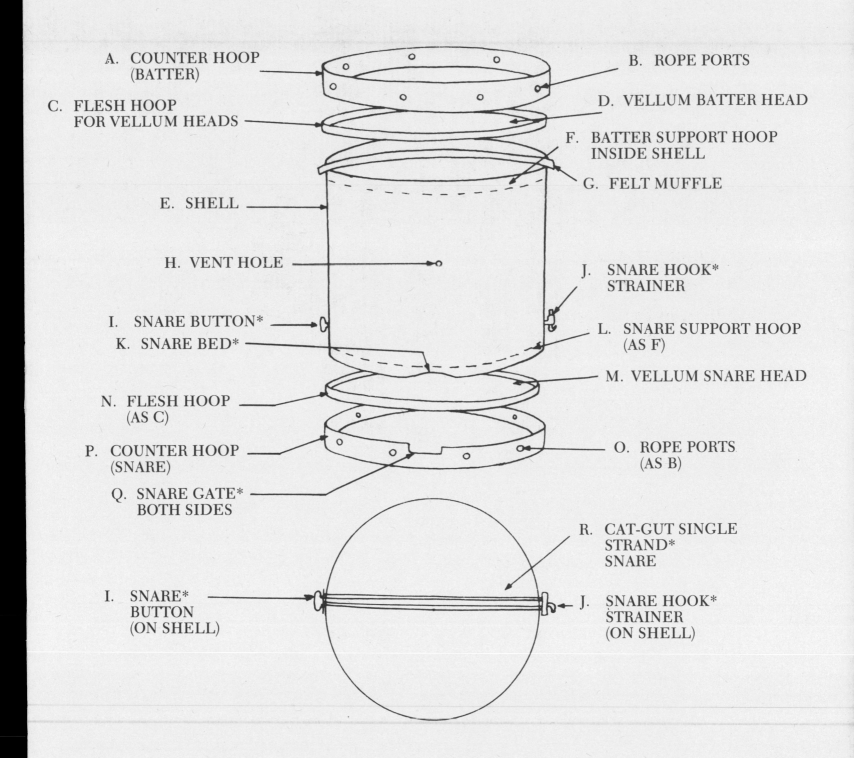

A. COUNTER HOOP
   (BATTER)

B. ROPE PORTS

C. FLESH HOOP
   FOR VELLUM HEADS

D. VELLUM BATTER HEAD

F. BATTER SUPPORT HOOP
   INSIDE SHELL

G. FELT MUFFLE

E. SHELL

H. VENT HOLE

J. SNARE HOOK*
   STRAINER

I. SNARE BUTTON*

K. SNARE BED*

L. SNARE SUPPORT HOOP
   (AS F)

M. VELLUM SNARE HEAD

N. FLESH HOOP
   (AS C)

P. COUNTER HOOP
   (SNARE)

O. ROPE PORTS
   (AS B)

Q. SNARE GATE*
   BOTH SIDES

R. CAT-GUT SINGLE
   STRAND*
   SNARE

I. SNARE*
   BUTTON
   (ON SHELL)

J. SNARE HOOK*
   STRAINER
   (ON SHELL)

*DOES NOT APPLY TO BASS DRUMS

7

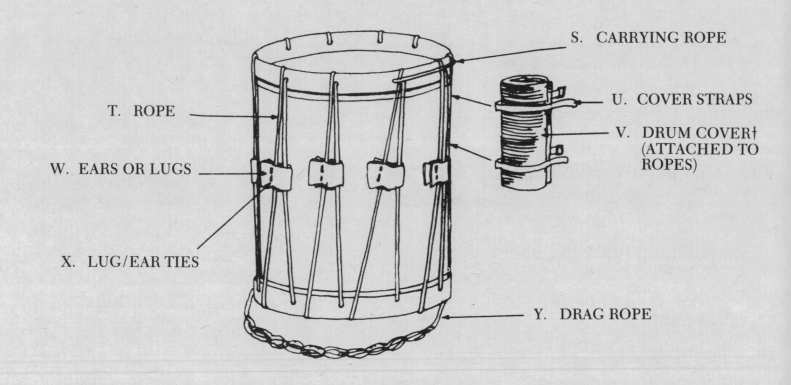

S. CARRYING ROPE

T. ROPE

U. COVER STRAPS

V. DRUM COVER†
(ATTACHED TO
ROPES)

W. EARS OR LUGS

X. LUG/EAR TIES

Y. DRAG ROPE

†DIFFERENT ATTACHMENT FOR BASS DRUMS

LESSON TWO
Holding the Drum Sticks

The left hand stick should rest in the hollow between the thumb and first finger and be held between the second and third fingers, palm upward. Pressure should be exerted between the thumb and the base of the index finger.

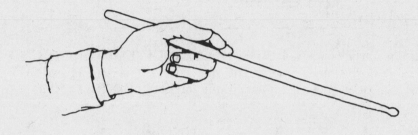

The right hand stick should be held between the thumb and first finger, palm downward, with the remaining fingers curled loosely around the stick. Pressure should be exerted between the thumb and the base of the index finger.

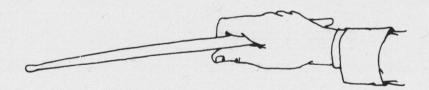

Both sticks should be held to produce a comfortable balance with the stick heads above the center of the drum head or drum pad.

LESSON THREE
Symbols

Now that you have learned to hold the sticks correctly, we will explain some of the symbols of music that you will need to learn.

A. The Staff or Stave

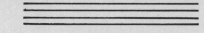

B. Bar or Measure Lines

Bar or measure lines are placed at regular intervals to space notes properly in a pattern.

C. Bass Clef Sign

All drum music is written in the F or bass clef. The term Clef is derived from the Latin word *clavis*, or key. The snare drum notes are placed in the third or E space in the bass clef. The bass drum notes are placed in the first or A space.

Snare Line
Bass Line

D. Treble Clef Sign

All fife music is written in the G or treble clef.

E. The Great Clef

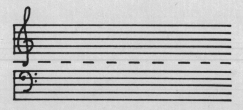

The example above shows the relative position of bass clef to treble clef.

F. Exercises:

1. Draw a staff.

2. Add three bar lines.

3. Insert clef symbols for drums.

4. Draw a staff with a treble clef.

5. Draw a great clef.

6. Name this symbol.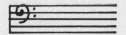

LESSON FOUR
Notes

A. Whole Note   A whole note has 4 counts.

  Half Note   A half note has 2 counts.

  Quarter Note   A quarter note has 1 count.

B. Examples of Value: Two quarter notes have the same time value as one half note, or

$$1 + 1 = 2$$

Four quarter notes have the same time value as one whole note, or

$$1 + 1 + 1 + 1 = 4$$

Two quarter notes and one half note have the same time value as one whole note, or

$$1 + 1 + 2 = 4$$

C. Exercises:
1. Draw a staff with five bar lines and a clef.

2. Insert four measures of time value using the notes explained, giving a four count value in each measure. Use the snare drum or E space.

3. Draw a staff, clef sign, bar lines, and notes for two proper measures of four count values in each measure. Use the bass drum or A space.

LESSON FIVE
Rests

For each written note value there is a corresponding rest symbol that equals the time alloted to the note.

A. Whole Rest   A whole rest receives the same value as one whole note

  Half Rest   A half rest receives the same value as one half note

  Quarter Rest   A quarter rest receives the same value as one quarter note

B. Examples of Value:

Two half note rests have the same value as one whole note rest, or

Two quarter note rests and one half note rest have the same value as one whole note rest, or

C. When notes and rests appear in the same measure, the value of each is counted.

Therefore, a quarter note, a quarter rest, and a half note rest have the same value as one whole note, or

You can mark this example as counts value

D. Exercises:

1. Draw a staff.

2. Add five measure lines.

3. Add the proper clef sign.

4. Make up four measures of drum beats, using notes and rests. Make sure that each measure contains four counts (both notes and rests) and that no two measures are the same.

LESSON SIX
First Rudiment

A. THE SINGLE STROKE is the basic movement of striking the center of the drum head with the stick when a note appears on the staff. To help you, each single stroke will be illustrated beneath the note by an L or an R for a left or a right stroke.

B. For Example:

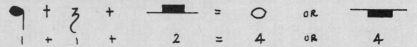

Each of the two measures is given a four count value.

C. Exercises:
Play the example above, using a wrist movement for both wrists to make the drum stick move up and down. Make sure that the stick head starts from a

position four inches above the drum or pad head, that it strikes the head only once, and that the stick head returns to its four-inch position once the stroke is completed.

Look at the number of symbols in each measure. The first measure contains four symbols. Give each symbol a number.

Count aloud slowly from one to four. As you count, execute a single stroke on count one with the left stick. Play nothing on count two. Execute a single stroke with the right stick on count three. Then play nothing on count four.

Check the following:
1. All counts should be of equal value or length.
2. The stick head should strike the center of the drum or pad head.
3. The wrist should move the stick down and up and strike the head only once. Should the stick bounce, exert a little more pressure at the grasping point.
4. The stick should not move during the rests.

Keep practicing the first measure until you are able to count evenly and control each stroke.

Look at the second measure. Check the number of symbols and give each a number.

Practice the second measure as you did the first and make the same checks.

Put both measures together. Remember that there is no gap between measures. Therefore you must play, in equal value or length:

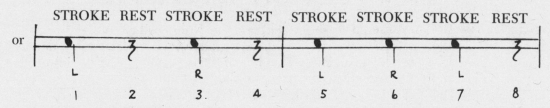

Now that you can read two measures of single strokes, write two measures of your own. Make sure that you:
1. Do not copy the same measures.
2. Have four counts value in each measure.
3. Check Lesson Five for notes and rests that can give you a four count value.
4. Insert the L or R below each note.
5. Insert the clef sign and measure lines.

PLEASE REFER TO THE FIRST LESSON ON THE RECORDING,
SIDE 1   BAND 2

LESSON SEVEN
Second Rudiment

A. THE FLAM is an effective note that is two strokes in rhythm, with no time value given to the shorter first note. A flam is played by striking the center of the drum head or pad with both sticks almost simultaneously. For your assistance, when a flam note appears on the staff, each flam will be illustrated beneath the note by an L or an R for a left or a right flam.

B. For Example:

Each of the two measures is given a four count value. The first flam is played as a light stroke R followed immediately by a heavy stroke L. Remember that no time value is given to the light stroke.

C. Exercises:
Play the example above using similar wrist movements, hand positions, and height above the drum head as you did with the single stroke. The two sticks should strike the center of the drum head one after the other, but almost together. The main stress should be on the second stroke of the flam.

Look at the number of symbols in each measure. The first measure contains four symbols, including the new symbol for a flam. Give each symbol a number.

Count aloud slowly from one to four. As you count, execute a flam on count one, using right stick to left stick. Play nothing on count two. Execute a flam on count three, using left stick to right stick. Play nothing on count four.

Check the following:
1. All counts should be of equal value. The first stroke of each flam has no time value.
2. The sticks should strike the center of the drum head or pad.
3. The wrists should move the sticks down and then up, and strike the head once only for each stick. Should the sticks bounce, exert a little more pressure at the grasping points as you did with the single stroke.
4. The sticks should not move during the rest counts.

Keep practicing the first measure until you are able to count evenly and control each flam.

Look at the second measure. Check the number of symbols and give each a number.

Practice the second measure as you did the first and make the same checks.

Put both measures together. Remember that there is no gap between measures. Therefore you must play in equal length:

Now that you can read two measures of flams, write two measures of your own. Make sure that you:
1. Do not copy the same measures.
2. Have four counts value in each measure.
3. Check Lessons Five and Six for notes and rests that can give you a four count value.
4. Insert L or R below each note.
5. Insert the clef sign and measure lines.

D. Practice:
You will now put single strokes and flams together in a practice piece. Remember to count aloud as you play.

Notice the difference in sound between a stroke and a flam.

Practice this exercise:

PLEASE REFER TO THE SECOND LESSON ON THE RECORDING,
SIDE 1   BAND 2

LESSON EIGHT
Notes and Rests

We will now add some more symbols to your present list.

A. Eighth note   An eighth note has a half count value.

Sixteenth note   A sixteenth note has a quarter count value.

Thirty-second note   A thirty-second note has an eighth count value.

B. Examples of Value:

Two eighth notes have the same time value as one quarter note, or

Two eighth notes and four sixteenth notes have the same time value as one half note, or

One quarter note, one eighth note, one sixteenth note, and two thirty-second notes have the same time value as one half note, or

C. For each written note value there is a corresponding rest symbol that equals the time alloted to the note.

An eighth note rest   receives the same value as an eighth note.

A sixteenth note rest ⅂ receives the same value as a sixteenth note.

A thirty-second note rest ⅀ receives the same value as a thirty-second note.

When notes and rests appear in the same measure, the value of each is counted.

D. Exercises:

Make up four measures of drum beats using notes and rests. Make sure that each measure contains four counts (both notes and rests) and that no two measures are the same. Make sure that you use both single strokes and flams for your drum beats. Always count the value of each symbol to arrive at four counts to each measure.

E. The following charts will help you to remember the values of each symbol that you have learned.

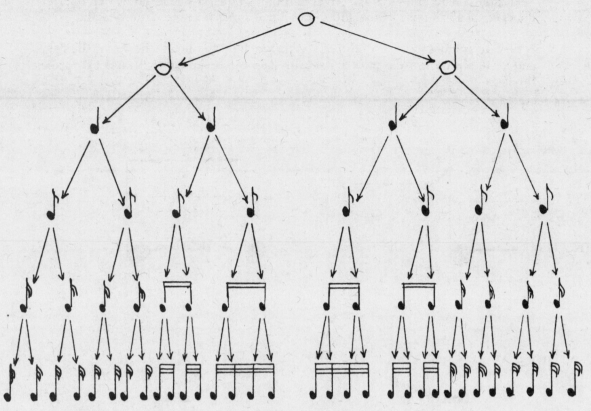

○ WHOLE NOTE	FOUR COUNTS	1
♩ HALF NOTE	TWO COUNTS	2
♩ QUARTER NOTE	ONE COUNT	4
♪ EIGHTH NOTE	HALF COUNT	8
♬ SIXTEENTH NOTE	QUARTER COUNT	16
♬ THIRTY-SECOND NOTE	EIGHTH COUNT	32

When two notes of the same value are combined, they will equal the value of the next largest note. For example, two half notes equal a whole note, two quarter notes equal a half note, two eighth notes equal a quarter note, and so forth.

Notes are composed of several parts, which include the head, the stem, the flag, and/or the beam. Two or more notes with flags can be joined by beams to replace the flags.

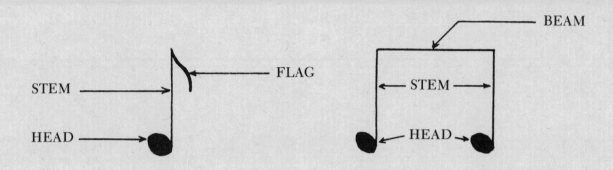

REST VALUES

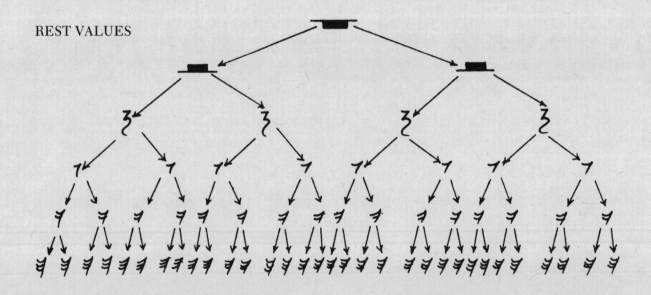

▬	WHOLE NOTE REST	FOUR COUNTS	1
▬	HALF NOTE REST	TWO COUNTS	2
𝄽	QUARTER NOTE REST	ONE COUNT	4
𝄾	EIGHTH NOTE REST	HALF COUNT	8
𝄿	SIXTEENTH NOTE REST	QUARTER COUNT	16
𝅀	THIRTY-SECOND NOTE REST	EIGHTH COUNT	32

LESSON NINE
Third Rudiment

A. THE RUFF. Similar to the flam, the ruff is an effective note that is three strokes in rhythm, with no time value given to the short first notes. A ruff is played by striking the center of the drum head or pad with both sticks almost simultaneously. When a ruff note appears on the staff, it will be illustrated beneath the note by an LL-R or an RR-L for right or left ruff.

B. For Example:

Each of the two measures is given a four count value. The first ruff is played as two light strokes RR followed immediately by a heavy stroke L. Remember that no time value is given to the first two light strokes.

C. Exercises: Play the example above. Use similar wrist movements, hand positions, and height above the drum head as you did with the single stroke and the flam. The two sticks should strike the center of the drum head one after the other, but almost together. The main stress should be on the third stroke of the ruff.

Look at the number of symbols in each measure. The first measure contains four symbols, including the new symbol for a ruff. Give each symbol a number.

Count aloud slowly from one to four. As you count, execute a ruff on count one, using two right strokes and one left stroke. Play nothing on count two. Execute a similar ruff on count three. Play nothing on count four.

Check the following:
1. All counts, rudiments, and rests should be of equal value. The first two strokes of each ruff have no time value.
2. The sticks should strike the center of the drum head or pad.
3. The wrists should move the sticks down and then up, and strike the head once only for each stroke.
4. The sticks should not move during the rest counts.

Keep playing the first measure until you are able to count evenly and control each ruff.

Look at the second measure. Check the number of symbols and give each a number.

Notice that the ruffs have now changed to two light strokes with the left stick followed immediately by a heavier stroke with the right stick. Practice the second measure as you did the first and make the same checks.

Put both measures together. Remember that there is no gap between measures. Therefore you must play in equal length:

Now that you can read two measures of ruffs, write two measures of your own. Make sure that you:

1. Do not copy the same measures.
2. Have four counts value in each measure.
3. Check Lessons Five, Six, and Eight for notes and rests that can give you a four count value.
4. Insert the L and R (known as sticking) below each note.
5. Insert the clef sign and measure lines.

D. Practice. We will now put single strokes, flams, and ruffs together in a practice piece. Remember to count aloud as you play.

Note the differences in sounds between strokes, flams, and ruffs. Practice this exercise:

1. Write in your own sticking (L and R).
2. Check that you can follow the sticking correctly.
3. Copy the above exercise in the space below.
4. Reverse the sticking.
5. Practice the exercise again.

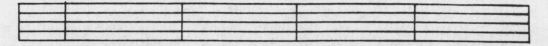

Exercises: All of the rudiment exercises you have practiced so far have contained only half note and quarter note values. Now you will add eighth and sixteenth note values to the measure patterns. Look at the following two measures, and follow the counts listed below:

Play a single stroke for each note and count aloud, using four counts for each measure. You will see that in the first measure, count one receives one stroke. Count two, which is of the same value, receives two strokes beaten in the same time as the first count. Count three receives one stroke, and count four receives two strokes. Help yourself to count by inserting "and" along with each of the eighth notes. The same two measures may look like this:

OR

OR

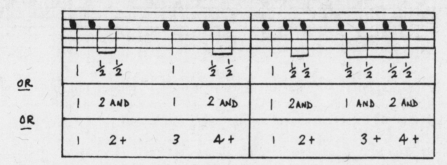

Write in the various counts and numbers under the following exercise.

COUNTS	1	2 etc.										
ADD "ANDS"	1	2 AND etc.										
ADD STICKING	L	R L etc.										
REVERSE STICKING	R	L R etc.										

PLEASE REFER TO LESSON 3 ON THE RECORDING, SIDE 1 BAND 2.

LESSON TEN
Fourth Rudiment

A. THE LONG ROLL. This is a most important rudiment and is the basis for all other rolls that are used. As with every other rudiment, but of more importance, the long roll should be practiced and mastered slowly, then speeded up *gradually* while maintaining control of every stroke. This exercise pattern is known as "open" and "close" and all rolls should be practiced "open," or slowly, then gradually quickened to "close," or fast, then gradually slowed to "open." The long roll consists of double strokes, that is, two strokes played by each hand, in succession

B. For Example:

This is the first rudiment you will learn that uses an unchanging pattern of double sticking, and while this may be the shortest exercise in the instructional booklet, it is the most crucial and requires the most practice.

C. Symbols. The symbol used for a roll is three diagonal lines drawn across the stem of the note. A number is written above the note to indicate the number of strokes to be played in the roll. A tie symbol is used to attach the first and last notes of the roll together. Thus:

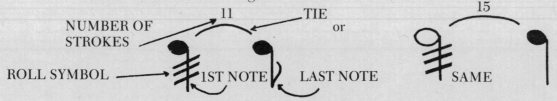

The first example, if written out in full, would look like this:

But it is easier for you to read:

D. Practice. Practice the long roll by beginning very slowly. When you make a mistake in the double stroke pattern of LL - RR - LL - RR, etc., stop and start again. Do not try to close the roll too soon.

PLEASE REFER TO LESSON 4 ON THE RECORDING, SIDE 1 BAND 3.

LESSON ELEVEN
Eighteenth-Century Duty Calls

A. Military Drummers of the seventeenth and eighteenth centuries were required to learn many signals and calls that could be used to replace voice commands during drills and on the field of battle. Using the rudiments you have already learned, begin to commit the following to memory. All are taken from *The Military Guide For Young Officers* by Thomas Grimes, published in 1776.

TURN OR FACE TO THE RIGHT

TURN OR FACE TO THE LEFT

WHEEL TO THE RIGHT

WHEEL TO THE LEFT

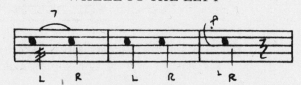

MAKE READY

WATER CALL

B. Exercises: Practice the above six exercises until you know them by heart. Do not always practice them in the same sequence. Make sure that you keep a steady count for each measure and that all symbols receive the correct time value.

LESSON TWELVE
Repeat and Double Bar Symbols

We will now add more symbols to your present list in order to simplify and condense written scores. Several symbols are used to denote repeating a measure or phrase or section that has already been written. The repeat symbols that you will most commonly encounter are the following:

A. 1. SINGLE MEASURE REPEAT SYMBOL

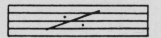

A diagonal line drawn *within* the measure, straddled by two dots. This symbol means play the measure immediately before it again. For example:

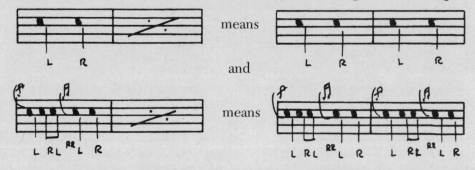

2. DOUBLE MEASURE REPEAT SYMBOL

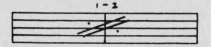

Diagonal lines drawn *across* two measures, straddled by two dots. This symbol means play the *two* measures immediately before it again. For example:

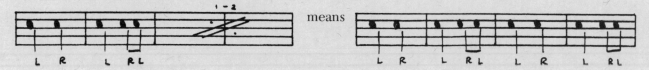

3. DOUBLE BAR SYMBOL

Music is divided into parts or sections. At the beginning and end of each section a double bar (or measure) line is used to help identify it. For example:

DOUBLE BAR LINES

The double bar line is used as a division. To further help you see the symbol, extra diagonal lines are sometimes added. For example:

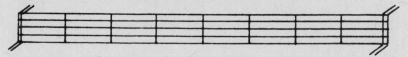

24

4. DOUBLE BAR REPEAT SYMBOL

Two dots placed within the staff spaces and within the double bar symbols.
Should the complete section or part need to be repeated, this symbol is used.
For example:

means

5. DA CAPO SYMBOL

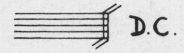

D.C., short for Da Capo, placed at the end of a written score means that
one goes back to the beginning and plays the score again. Da Capo is an
Italian phrase meaning "to the head." This example of a repeat symbol
precludes having to write the complete score a second time.

B. Exercises:

    a. Draw a staff above.
    b. Add a clef sign.
    c. Draw enough measure lines for eight measures.
    d. Insert the proper strokes for one measure.
    e. Make sure that you have the correct count.
    f. Draw a single measure repeat symbol behind your first measure.
    g. Insert the proper strokes for two measures.
    h. Make sure that you have the correct count.
    j. Draw a double measure repeat symbol behind the third and fourth measures.
    k. Complete the last two measures by inserting proper strokes.
    l. Make sure that you have the correct count.
    m. Draw double bar lines at the beginning and the end of the eight measures.
    n. Insert double bar repeat symbols.
    o. Insert a D.C. symbol.
    p. Add sticking L and R.
    q. Count carefully—you have put actual notes in only five measures. How many measures can you play if you follow all of the repeat symbols in your score? The answer should be thirty-two. This example will show you how helpful repeat symbols can be.

LESSON THIRTEEN
Fifth Rudiment

A. THE FIVE-STROKE ROLL. One of the more common rudiments used in drumming, the five-stroke roll should be practiced and mastered slowly in an open and closed pattern while maintaining control of every stroke. As do all other rolls, the five-stroke roll consists of double strokes.

B. Symbols. You will learn two symbols with this rudiment. The first was explained in Lesson Ten. The second is a stress or accent symbol, showing a heavier stroke than other strokes in the pattern. Thus:

This example, if written out in full, would look like this:

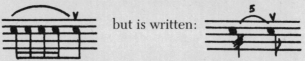

The stress symbol tells you to accent the final stroke.

C. For Example:

D. Practice. Practice the five-stroke rolls by beginning very slowly. Notice that they always start and end on the same stick. Also notice that they are written hand-to-hand for this practice, i.e., LL - RR - L - RR - LL - R. You should be able to play either pattern equally well. Do not try to close the five-stroke rolls too soon.

E. Exercises: Play the following. Make sure that you can control every stroke in the rolls.

Once you can play this correctly, reverse the sticking and practice again.

PLEASE REFER TO LESSON 5 ON THE RECORDING,
SIDE 1   BAND 3

LESSON FOURTEEN
Time Signatures

A. EXPLANATION. In Lesson Four, a value of counts and numbers was assigned to each note, as follows:

◯	Whole Note	(1)	Four counts each
♩	Half Note	(2)	Two counts each
♩	Quarter Note	(4)	One count each
♪	Eighth Note	(8)	Half count each
♬	Sixteenth Note	(16)	Quarter count each
♬	Thirty-second Note	(32)	Eighth count each

Study the number in parentheses above in order to understand time signatures, which appear on every score immediately following the clef sign. Time signatures are composed of two numbers, one above the other. For example:

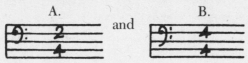

A.   and   B.

In a time signature, the upper number represents the amount of counts in the measures following and the lower number represents the value of the notes in the measures following.

B. For Example: In example A you can see $\frac{2}{4}$. The two equals two counts, and the four equals quarter notes (refer to the Explanation above). Therefore, $\frac{2}{4}$ equals two quarter notes value in each measure. Please note that it represents two quarter notes VALUE. This means that any combination of notes and/or rests that add up to the value of two quarter notes is correct in value.

In example B you can see $\frac{4}{4}$. The upper four equals four counts, and the lower four equals quarter notes. Therefore $\frac{4}{4}$ equals four quarter notes (and/or rests) value in each measure.

C. Exercises: Using only the two time signatures already discussed, check the following exercises and mark which is correct IN VALUE and which is not.

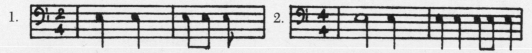

To help you count, insert the count numbers below the notes, then add the total for each measure as follows:

correct   incorrect

D. For Example: You should now understand the formula for finding correct values for time signatures.

2 / 4	two quarter note	values in each measure
4 / 4	four quarter note	values in each measure

Remember that rest values *must* be included.

Look at other time signatures.

3 / 4	three quarter note	values in each measure

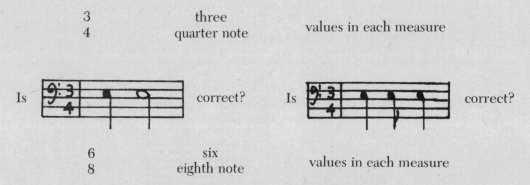

6 / 8	six eighth note	values in each measure

This is the first example of a different lower note in the time signature. The lower 8 means eighth note values as shown in parenthesis in your value table.

$\frac{4}{4}$ is called Common Time and is often written in a time signature like this:

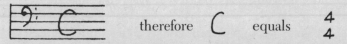 therefore C equals $\frac{4}{4}$

$\frac{2}{2}$ is also called Half-common Time or cut time and is often written in a time signature like this:

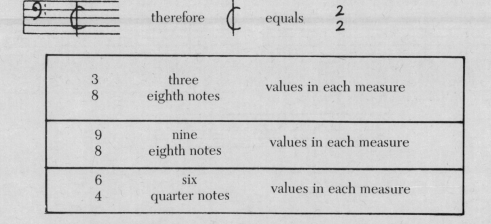 therefore $\cent$ equals $\frac{2}{2}$

3 / 8	three eighth notes	values in each measure
9 / 8	nine eighth notes	values in each measure
6 / 4	six quarter notes	values in each measure

E. Exercises: Insert the correct time signature into the following exercises. Make sure that you count *all* of the notes and rests values in the measures.

Insert correct values for the following time signatures. Try to use notes *and* rests.

LESSON FIFTEEN
Sixth and Seventh Rudiments

A. THE SEVEN-STROKE ROLL
            and
B. THE FIFTEEN-STROKE ROLL

As with the five-stroke roll in Lesson Thirteen, these two rudiments should be practiced and mastered slowly in an open and closed pattern while maintaining control of every stroke.

C. Symbols.

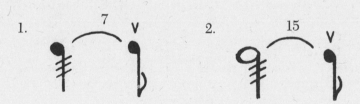

These examples, if written out in full, would look like this:

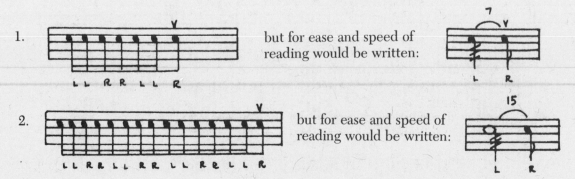

The stress symbols tell you to accent the final stroke.
If there is no stress symbol, do not accent the final stroke.

D. For Example:

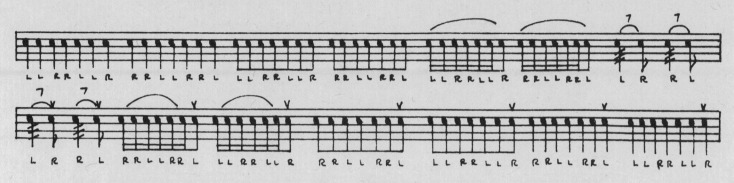

2.

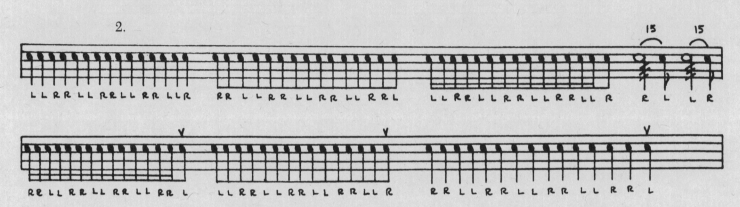

E. Practice. Using both seven- and fifteen-stroke rolls, begin slowly and gradually increase the tempo, making sure that every stroke is given equal time and emphasis. Notice that, unlike the five-stroke rolls, both the seven- and fifteen-stroke rolls start and finish with opposite sticks. Both new rudiments should be practiced in either pattern. For example,
1. LL-RR-LL-R and RR-LL-RR-L.
2. LL-RR-LL-RR-LL-RR-LL-R and RR-LL-RR-LL-RR-LL-RR-L.

F. Exercises:
Play the following.
Make sure that you do not disregard any other written rudiment in the exercise and that you can control every stroke in every roll.

Once you can play this correctly, reverse the sticking and practice again.

What time signature is used in the above exercise?
What other time signature could be used?

PLEASE REFER TO LESSON 6 ON THE RECORDING, SIDE 1 BAND 3.

LESSON SIXTEEN
Eighth Rudiment

A. THE PARADIDDLE. An effective pattern of single strokes, in rhythm, each of equal value, the paradiddle is designed to ensure smoothness of flow of strokes. As with other rudiments, the sticking will be inserted for you.

B. For example:

You will see that the paradiddle, which is a phonetic description of the pattern, has a definite sticking movement. Unless otherwise written with accents, each stroke receives equal time, value , and stress.

It is important that you can play either stroke evenly. The transition from one pattern (L-R-L-L) to another (R-L-R-R) is equally important. Do not progress until you are satisfied that each stroke and the transition is smooth and even.

C. Exercises: Play the above example, but reverse the sticking pattern so that you can play R-L-R-R-L-R-L-L. Make sure that you do not change tempo during the exercise. Make sure that your wrist movements are correct, that the height of the sticks from the head is even, and that you strike the center of the drum head.

D. Practice. We will now increase the tempo of the paradiddle by the following:

When you are comfortable with the repeated pattern, then reverse the sticking and practice again.

In order to increase your interdependence and coordination, practice the paradiddle by tapping your feet, in tempo, using the pattern already described.

We will now further increase the tempo.

Reverse the sticking pattern and practice again.

E. Further Exercises: We will now add some accents for you to interpret and play.

As with all the other exercises, once you have played it properly, reverse the sticking and practice again.

Place the accent elsewhere.

Reverse the sticking.

Place the accents in differing patterns.

Reverse the sticking.

Play the following. This will allow you to practice going into and coming out of the paradiddle rudiment to and from other rudiments.

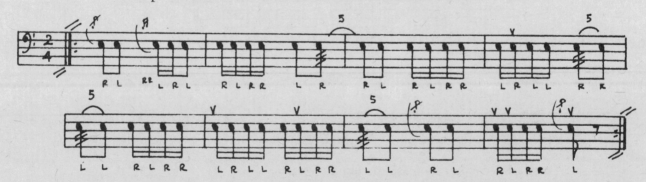

Do not progress until you are able to complete the above exercise properly. Check your tempo and stresses. Once completed, reverse the sticking.

Write two measures of $\frac{2}{4}$ score using at least one paradiddle rudiment. Insert the sticking. Check each measure for value, then practice.

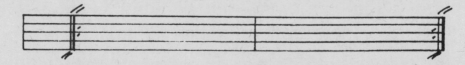

PLEASE REFER TO LESSON 7 ON THE RECORDING, SIDE 2 BAND 1.

LESSON SEVENTEEN
Repertoire Scores

By this time you should be able to read, interpret, and play some simple drum scores. The following are examples designed to be helpful and useful. Most of the rudiments and exercises already included in previous lessons are used in these scores.

As with every other exercise, do not proceed until you are completely satisfied with your performance. Marks of dynamic expression, which will be discussed in Lesson Nineteen, have not been included in the following scores.

1. Make sure that you read each measure.

2. Execute all of the stress marks written.

3. Check your tempo of playing constantly.

4. Ensure that every roll you play contains the written number of strokes.

5. Check the execution of each flam and ruff written.

6. Remember that the rest symbols are as important as the note symbols.

7. Do not be satisfied with a fair performance. Your goal should be perfection of every symbol written in the score.

8. In the score of "Chester" there appears a symbol that has not yet been discussed. Can you find that symbol? Lesson Nineteen will explain this new symbol.

PLEASE REFER TO LESSON 8 ON THE RECORDING, SIDE 2 BAND 1.

CHESTER

SNARE DRUM   COLONIAL WILLIAMSBURG FIFES & DRUMS   By Buck Soistman
Va. State Garrison Regt.   1963

THE WHITE COCKADE

By John C. Moon
1973

34

CHESTER

BASS DRUM

COLONIAL WILLIAMSBURG FIFES & DRUMS
Va. State Garrison Regt.

By Buck Soistman
1963

THE WHITE COCKADE

By John C. Moon
1973

LESSON EIGHTEEN
Ninth and Tenth Rudiments

A. THE NINE-STROKE ROLL
          and
B. THE ELEVEN-STROKE ROLL

As with the previous rolls, these two rudiments should be practiced and mastered slowly in an open and closed pattern while maintaining control of every stroke.

C. Symbols.

These symbols, if written out in full, would look like this:

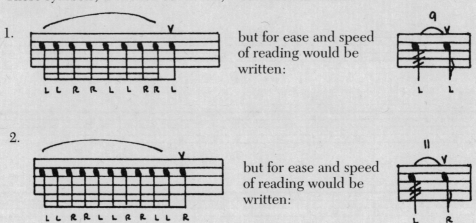

but for ease and speed of reading would be written:

but for ease and speed of reading would be written:

The stress symbols tell you to accent the final stroke.
If there is no stress symbol, do not accent the final stroke.

D. For Example:

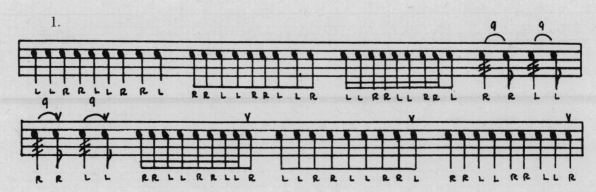

2.

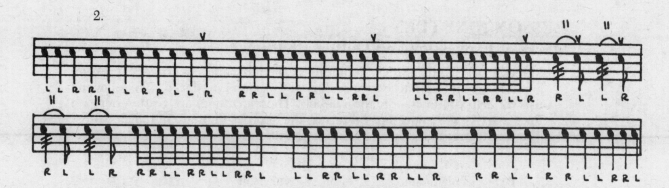

E. Practice. Using both nine- and eleven-stroke rolls, begin slowly and gradually increase the tempo, making sure that every stroke is given equal time and emphasis. Notice that the nine-stroke roll starts and finishes on the same stick, and that the eleven-stroke roll starts and finishes on opposite sticks. Both rudiments should be practiced in either pattern.
For example:

1. LL-RR-LL-RR-L   and   RR-LL-RR-LL-R
2. LL-RR-LL-RR-LL-R   and   RR-LL-RR-LL-RR-L

F. Exercises: Play the following. Make sure that you play all other rudiments properly and that you can control every stroke in every roll.

You will notice that, while the time signature and the tempo remain constant, you must execute the nines and the elevens in slightly different tempi, the nines being more open than the elevens.

Once you can play this correctly, reverse the sticking and practice again.

Play the following roles in succession.

Practice the same exercise and add a stress to each ending note.

Reverse the sticking pattern and practice again both with and without final stresses.

PLEASE REFER TO LESSON 9 ON THE RECORDING, SIDE 2 BAND 1.

LESSON NINETEEN
Marks of Expression and Dotted Rhythms

A. MARKS OF EXPRESSION. Sometimes called dynamics, marks of expression are used to indicate musical expression of the sound produced. The following list will help you to identify the symbols. These markings are written beneath the stave. As with most musical terms, the abbreviations are of Italian words. The list gives both Italian and English definitions.

1. *pp*   pianissimo   or   very soft

     p   piano   or   soft

     mp   mezzo piano   or   moderately soft

     mf   mezzo forte   or   moderately loud

     f   forte   or   loud

     ff   fortissimo   or   very loud

Some composers and arrangers also use *ppp* and *fff* The meaning of these symbols should be obvious.

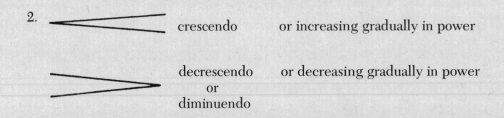

2.   crescendo   or increasing gradually in power

     decrescendo   or decreasing gradually in power
     or
     diminuendo

3. You have already used the stress or attack symbol ᵛ placed above any note that is to be accented.

All marks of expression are vital to good drumming, whether individually or in unison. Failure to recognize and execute dynamics results in a flat, boring rendition that will become monotonous.

B. DOTTED RHYTHMS. A dot placed after any note will add half of its value to that note.
Thus:

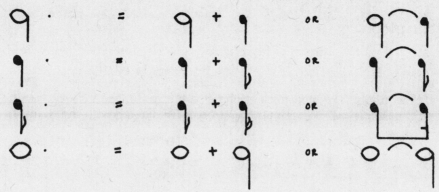

Similarly, a dot placed behind any rest increases its value by half. Thus:

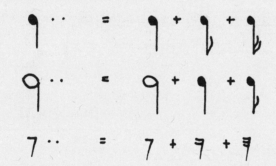

In rare cases double dots are used. A double dot after a note or rest increases its value by a half plus a quarter. Thus:

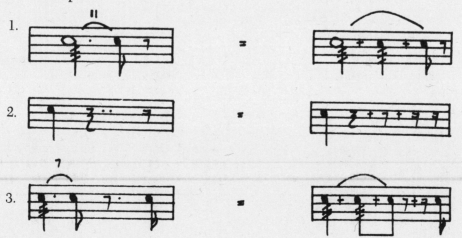

C. For Example:

1.

2.

3.

Study these examples and then insert a time signature that would be correct for each. Remember to count the values of notes, dots, and rests.

LESSON TWENTY
Triplets

A. A triplet is a group of three notes, or rests, to be performed in the time that two notes or rests of the same value would ordinarily take.

B. Symbols. The sign for a triplet is a figure 3 placed above the three notes to be so played. Sometimes a bracket is used along with the figure three.

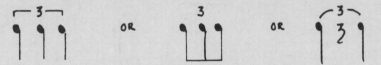

C. For Example: The value of time does not change, therefore:

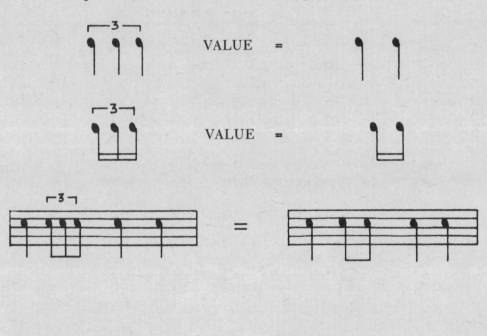

D. SIXES or DOUBLE TRIPLETS. This requires six notes or rests to be performed in the time that four notes or rests of the same value would ordinarily take.

E. For Example:

Again, the value does not change, therefore:

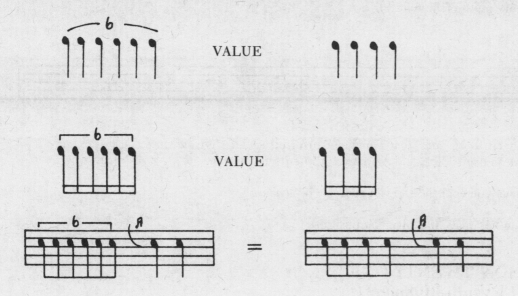

F. Exercises:

Notice that the triplets are played hand-to-hand. Reverse the sticking and practice again.

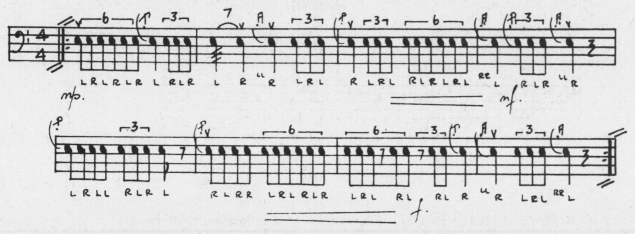

Change the sticking and practice again.

Here is an opportunity to compose a four measure drum beating. Write your score on the following stave.

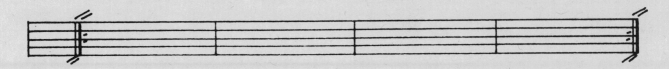

Check to be sure that you have inserted a clef sign, accents, and sticking. Try to use triplets and as many rudiments as you can.

A. Have you counted the values in each measure?

B. Can you play your own composition?

LESSON TWENTY-ONE
The Eleventh Rudiment

A. THE SINGLE RATAMACUE. This rudiment is a combination of notes played in strict rhythm, with no time value given to the short first notes, or ruff. The sticking for the ratamacue is written and played hand-to-hand with the exception of the opening ruff.

B. For example:

Each single ratamacue starts and finishes on the same stick. Remember that no time value is given to the opening ruff. The three eighth notes are played in time of two eighth notes.

C. Exercises:

Once you have perfected the ratamacue rhythm, reverse the sticking and practice again.

D. DOUBLE RATAMACUE. This rudiment is effected by playing a ruff before the single ratamacue. Thus:

Each double ratamacue starts and finishes on the same stick.

E. **TRIPLE RATAMACUE.** This rudiment is effected by playing two ruffs before the single ratamacue. Thus:

Each triple ratamacue starts and finishes on the same stick.

F. Exercises: The following exercise incorporates the rudiments that you have already learned. Practice the exercise slowly so that you can move from rudiment to rudiment with ease. Once you feel satisfied with your performance, insert sticking that will allow you to play smoothly.

Once you have inserted the sticking, study the exercise, then insert marks of expression that might help the dynamic sounds of the exercise.

Reverse the sticking and practice again.

Write down the names of rudiments in the exercise that you recognize.

**PLEASE REFER TO LESSON 10 ON THE RECORDING,
SIDE 2   BAND 2**

LESSON TWENTY-TWO
Repertoire Scores

To continue to practice your reading ability, the following repertoire scores will give you experience and an opportunity to improve your playing technique.

1. Pay strict attention to all of the stress marks and marks of expression.

2. Check your tempo of playing constantly.

3. Execute the proper sticking.

4. Do not be satisfied with a fair performance. Your goal should be perfection of every symbol written in the score.

5. Practice the marches and open beating until you know them completely and can play them without the score.

PLEASE REFER TO LESSON 11 ON THE RECORDING,
SIDE 2   BAND 2

FIRST TURK'S MARCH

SNARE DRUM
COLONIAL WILLIAMSBURG FIFES & DRUMS
Va. State Garrison Regt.

To fit Beck MS ca 1780
By John C. Moon

COUNTRY DANCE

To fit Fifer's Companion ca 1804
by John C. Moon

OPEN BEATING Nº. 3

Adapted by John C. Moon

FIRST TURK'S MARCH

BASS DRUM
COLONIAL WILLIAMSBURG FIFES & DRUMS
Va. State Garrison Regt.

To fit Beck MS ca 1780

COUNTRY DANCE

To fit Fifer's Companion ca. 1804
by John C. Moon

OPEN BEATING Nº. 3

Adapted by John C. Moon

LESSON TWENTY-THREE
Twelfth Rudiment

A. THE DOUBLE PARADIDDLE. The double paradiddle is a pattern of single strokes in rhythm, each of equal value, designed to ensure smoothness of flow.

B. For Example:

The double paradiddle has a definite sticking pattern and, unless otherwise written with accents, each stroke receives equal time, value and stress. You will find that the double paradiddle is a useful rudiment when playing in ¾ or ⁶/₈ time signatures.

It is important to play each stroke evenly. The transition from one pattern (L - R - L - R - L - L) to another (R - L - R - L - R - R) is equally important. Do not progress until you are satisfied that each stroke and the pattern transition is smooth and even.

C. Exercises:

Reverse the sticking and practice again.

Reverse the sticking and practice again.

D. Practice. As with the paradiddle, practice the double paradiddle by tapping your feet in tempo using the pattern already described.

We will now add some accents for you to interpret and play.

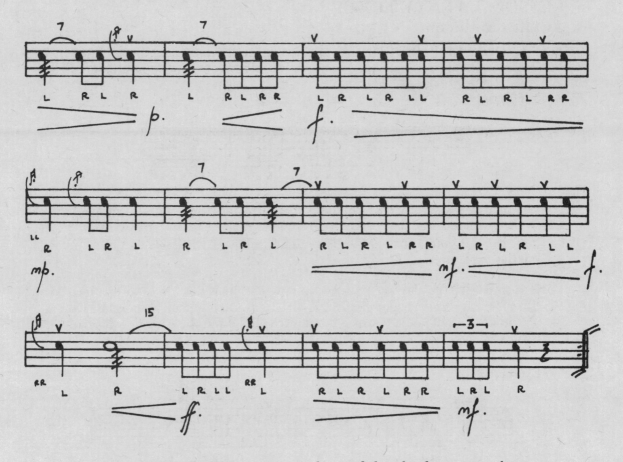

a. Be sure that all of the accents are clear and that the dynamic markings are played properly.
b. Check your tempo constantly.
c. Be sure that you make use of the double paradiddle rudiment wherever applicable.
d. Reverse the sticking and practice again.

PLEASE REFER TO LESSON 12 ON THE RECORDING,
SIDE 2   BAND 3

LESSON TWENTY-FOUR
Thirteenth Rudiment

A. THE FLAMACUE. The flamacue is a pattern of flams and single strokes in rhythm, each of equal value, designed to start and finish with a flam stroke and with an accent on the second beat.

B. For Example:

The flamacue starts and finishes on opposite sticks. It is important that you can execute the flammacue by using either sticking.

C. Exercises:

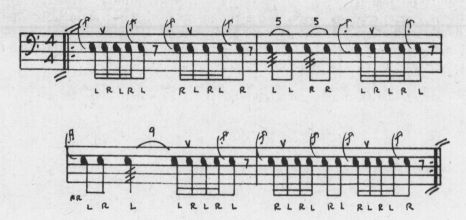

Reverse the sticking and practice again.

D. Practice. Try to recognize each flamacue in the following score and be sure that your sticking remains constant to the rudiment.

Reverse the sticking and practice again.

PLEASE REFER TO LESSON 13 ON THE RECORDING, SIDE 2 BAND 3

Once you have reached this stage and feel satisfied with your understanding and execution of the rudiments and practices, you may consider yourself an apprentice drummer.

Remember that there is no substitute for daily practice and experience in reading. If you cannot read and perform the rudiments in this instructional booklet, you should re-study the lessons that you feel are required. Should you not feel comfortable with any of the patterns, you must continue to study and practice them. Otherwise, the only person you fool will be yourself.

All rudimentary drumming roads are now open for you to discover and explore.